OFFICIAL

TEENAGER

> *"keep taking chances - make life a beautiful experience and never give up!"*

Date: /   /

_____

_____

_____

_____

_____

_____

_____

_____

_____

_____

_____

_____

_____

_____

_____

_____

_____

_____

_____

_____

_____

THINGS TO BE GRATEFUL FOR TODAY

"Have dreams and dream big! Dream without fear"

Date: /   /

THINGS TO BE GRATEFUL FOR TODAY

"Believe in miracles but above all believe in yourself!"

Date: /   /

THINGS TO BE GRATEFUL FOR TODAY

"Let your dreams be as big as your desire to succeed"

Date: /   /

THINGS TO BE GRATEFUL FOR TODAY

> *"Never downgrade your dreams, reach for the stars and believe in your self power"*

Date: /   /

_____

_____

_____

_____

_____

_____

_____

_____

_____

_____

_____

_____

_____

_____

_____

_____

_____

_____

THINGS TO BE GRATEFUL FOR TODAY

Date: /   /

_____

_____

_____

_____

_____

_____

_____

_____

_____

_____

_____

_____

_____

_____

_____

_____

_____

_____

THINGS TO BE GRATEFUL FOR TODAY

> *"Never be afraid to start something new,*
> *if you fail it is just temporary, if you believe*
> *and persist you will succeed"*

Date: /   /

THINGS TO BE GRATEFUL FOR TODAY

Date: /   /

_____

_____

_____

_____

_____

_____

_____

_____

_____

_____

_____

_____

_____

_____

_____

_____

_____

_____

THINGS TO BE GRATEFUL FOR TODAY

"Wherever you go, go with all your heart."
- Confucius

Date: /   /

THINGS TO BE GRATEFUL FOR TODAY

> *"Build your own dreams or you will end up building someone else's dreams"*

Date: /   /

THINGS TO BE GRATEFUL FOR TODAY

> *"Your dreams and your goals are the seeds of your own success"*

Date: /   /

_____

THINGS TO BE GRATEFUL FOR TODAY

"Never give up, keep going no matter what!"

Date: /   /

THINGS TO BE GRATEFUL FOR TODAY

Date: /   /

THINGS TO BE GRATEFUL FOR TODAY

> *"If you never give up you become unbeatable, just keep going!"*

Date: /   /

_____
_____
_____
_____
_____
_____
_____
_____
_____
_____
_____
_____
_____
_____
_____
_____
_____
_____
_____

THINGS TO BE GRATEFUL FOR TODAY

"Life isn't about finding yourself. Life is about creating yourself." - George Bernard Shaw

Date: /   /

THINGS TO BE GRATEFUL FOR TODAY

> *"Change your life today. Don't gamble on the future, act now, without delay."* — *Simone de Beauvoir*

Date: /   /

THINGS TO BE GRATEFUL FOR TODAY

Date: /   /

THINGS TO BE GRATEFUL FOR TODAY

"Aim for the stars to keep your dreams alive"

Date: /   /

_____
_____
_____
_____
_____
_____
_____
_____
_____
_____
_____
_____
_____
_____
_____
_____
_____
_____
_____

THINGS TO BE GRATEFUL FOR TODAY

"When life gives you lemons, add a little gin and tonic"

Date: /   /

THINGS TO BE GRATEFUL FOR TODAY

Date: /   /

THINGS TO BE GRATEFUL FOR TODAY

> *"When you feel you are defeated, just remember, you have the power to move on, it is all in your mind"*

Date: /   /
_____

_____

_____

_____

_____

_____

_____

_____

_____

_____

_____

_____

_____

_____

_____

_____

_____

_____

THINGS TO BE GRATEFUL FOR TODAY

"Don't just dream your dreams, make them happen!"

Date: /   /

_____

_____

_____

_____

_____

_____

_____

_____

_____

_____

_____

_____

_____

_____

_____

_____

_____

_____

_____

THINGS TO BE GRATEFUL FOR TODAY

"Opportunity comes to those who never give up"

Date: /   /

THINGS TO BE GRATEFUL FOR TODAY

Date: /   /

THINGS TO BE GRATEFUL FOR TODAY

Date: /   /

_____

_____

_____

_____

_____

_____

_____

_____

_____

_____

_____

_____

_____

_____

_____

_____

_____

_____

_____

THINGS TO BE GRATEFUL FOR TODAY

Date: /   /

THINGS TO BE GRATEFUL FOR TODAY

Date: /   /

THINGS TO BE GRATEFUL FOR TODAY

Date: /   /

_____
_____
_____
_____
_____
_____
_____
_____
_____
_____
_____
_____
_____
_____
_____
_____

THINGS TO BE GRATEFUL FOR TODAY

"Never loose confidence in your dreams, there will be obstacles and defeats, but you will always win if you persist"

Date: /   /

THINGS TO BE GRATEFUL FOR TODAY

Date: /   /

THINGS TO BE GRATEFUL FOR TODAY

"Dreams are the energy that power your life"

Date: /   /

_____

_____

_____

_____

_____

_____

_____

_____

_____

_____

_____

_____

_____

_____

_____

_____

_____

_____

_____

THINGS TO BE GRATEFUL FOR TODAY

"Dreams make things happen, nothing is impossible as long as you believe." - Anonymous

Date: /   /

THINGS TO BE GRATEFUL FOR TODAY

Date: /   /

THINGS TO BE GRATEFUL FOR TODAY

"Never stop dreaming." - Anonymous

Date: / /

THINGS TO BE GRATEFUL FOR TODAY

> *"Everything you dream is possible as long as you believe in yourself"*

Date: /   /

_____

THINGS TO BE GRATEFUL FOR TODAY

"Dream big, it's the first step to success" - Anonymous

Date: /   /

THINGS TO BE GRATEFUL FOR TODAY

Date: /   /

THINGS TO BE GRATEFUL FOR TODAY

"Motivation comes from working on our dreams and from taking action to achieve our goals"

Date: / /

THINGS TO BE GRATEFUL FOR TODAY

Date: /   /

THINGS TO BE GRATEFUL FOR TODAY

> *"Your mission in life should be to thrive and not merely survive"*

Date: /   /

_____

_____

_____

_____

_____

_____

_____

_____

_____

_____

_____

_____

_____

_____

_____

_____

_____

THINGS TO BE GRATEFUL FOR TODAY

> *"Doing what you believe in, and going after your dreams will only result in success."* - Anonymous

Date: /   /
_____

_____
_____
_____
_____
_____
_____
_____
_____
_____
_____
_____
_____
_____
_____
_____
_____
_____
_____

THINGS TO BE GRATEFUL FOR TODAY

"The right time to start something new is now"

Date: /   /
_____

_____
_____
_____
_____
_____
_____
_____
_____
_____
_____
_____
_____
_____
_____
_____
_____
_____
_____
_____

THINGS TO BE GRATEFUL FOR TODAY

> *"Be brave, fight for what you believe in and make your dreams a reality."* - Anonymous

Date: /   /

_____

_____

_____

_____

_____

_____

_____

_____

_____

_____

_____

_____

_____

_____

_____

_____

_____

_____

_____

THINGS TO BE GRATEFUL FOR TODAY

> *"Put more energy into your dreams than
> Into your fears and you will see positive results"*

Date: /   /

THINGS TO BE GRATEFUL FOR TODAY

"Let your dreams be bigger than your fears and your actions louder than your words." - Anonymous

Date: /   /

THINGS TO BE GRATEFUL FOR TODAY

> *"Always keep moving forward to keep your balance, if you stop dreaming you will fall"*

Date: /   /

THINGS TO BE GRATEFUL FOR TODAY

> *"Start every day with a goal in mind and make it happen with your actions"*

Date: /   /

_____

_____

_____

_____

_____

_____

_____

_____

_____

_____

_____

_____

_____

_____

_____

_____

_____

_____

THINGS TO BE GRATEFUL FOR TODAY

"Dream. Believe. Create. Succeed" - Anonymous

Date: /   /

_____

_____

_____

_____

_____

_____

_____

_____

_____

_____

_____

_____

_____

_____

_____

_____

_____

_____

THINGS TO BE GRATEFUL FOR TODAY

"You are never to old to set new goals and achieve them, keep on dreaming!"

Date: /   /

THINGS TO BE GRATEFUL FOR TODAY

> *"If you have big dreams you will always have big reasons to wake up every day"*

Date: /   /

_____

_____

_____

_____

_____

_____

_____

_____

_____

_____

_____

_____

_____

_____

_____

_____

_____

THINGS TO BE GRATEFUL FOR TODAY

"Difficulties are nothing more than opportunities in disguise, keep on trying and you will succeed"

Date:　　　/　　　/

THINGS TO BE GRATEFUL FOR TODAY

> *"To achieve our dreams we must first overcome our fear of failure"*

Date: /   /

THINGS TO BE GRATEFUL FOR TODAY

> *"Always have a powerful reason to wake up every new morning, set goals and follow your dreams"*

Date: /   /

_____

_____

_____

_____

_____

_____

_____

_____

_____

_____

_____

_____

_____

_____

_____

_____

_____

_____

_____

_____

THINGS TO BE GRATEFUL FOR TODAY

"Use failure as a motivation tool not as a sign of defeat"

Date: /   /

_____
_____
_____
_____
_____
_____
_____
_____
_____
_____
_____
_____
_____
_____
_____
_____
_____
_____
_____

THINGS TO BE GRATEFUL FOR TODAY

*"Never let your dreams die for fear of failure,
defeat is just temporary; your dreams are your power"*

Date: /   /

THINGS TO BE GRATEFUL FOR TODAY

> *"A failure is a lesson, not a loss. It is a temporary and sometimes necessary detour, not a dead end"*

Date: /   /

_____

_____

_____

_____

_____

_____

_____

_____

_____

_____

_____

_____

_____

_____

_____

_____

_____

_____

_____

THINGS TO BE GRATEFUL FOR TODAY

"Have faith in the future but above all in yourself"

Date: /   /

_____

_____

_____

_____

_____

_____

_____

_____

_____

_____

_____

_____

_____

_____

_____

_____

_____

_____

THINGS TO BE GRATEFUL FOR TODAY

Date: /   /

THINGS TO BE GRATEFUL FOR TODAY

Date: /   /

THINGS TO BE GRATEFUL FOR TODAY

"Never let your doubt blind your goals, for your future lies in your ability, not your failure" — Anonymous

Date: /   /

THINGS TO BE GRATEFUL FOR TODAY

Date: /   /

THINGS TO BE GRATEFUL FOR TODAY

> *"Laughter is the shock absorber that softens and minimizes the bumps of life" — Anonymous*

Date: /   /

_____

_____

_____

_____

_____

_____

_____

_____

_____

_____

_____

_____

_____

_____

_____

_____

_____

_____

_____

THINGS TO BE GRATEFUL FOR TODAY

"Dream – Believe – Achieve"

Date: /   /

_____

_____

_____

_____

_____

_____

_____

_____

_____

_____

_____

_____

_____

_____

_____

_____

_____

_____

_____

THINGS TO BE GRATEFUL FOR TODAY

> *"Make your own destiny. Don't wait for it to come to you, life is not a rehearsal"* — Anonymous

Date: /   /

THINGS TO BE GRATEFUL FOR TODAY

Date: /   /

_____

_____

_____

_____

_____

_____

_____

_____

_____

_____

_____

_____

_____

_____

_____

_____

_____

_____

THINGS TO BE GRATEFUL FOR TODAY

"Never give up on a dream just because of the time it will take to accomplish it. The time will pass anyway." – Anonymous

Date: /   /

THINGS TO BE GRATEFUL FOR TODAY

"I am never a failure until I begin blaming others"
- Anonymous

Date: /   /

_____

_____

_____

_____

_____

_____

_____

_____

_____

_____

_____

_____

_____

_____

_____

_____

_____

_____

_____

THINGS TO BE GRATEFUL FOR TODAY

"Your only limitation is your imagination" — *Anonymous*

Date: /   /

_____
_____
_____
_____
_____
_____
_____
_____
_____
_____
_____
_____
_____
_____
_____
_____
_____
_____
_____

THINGS TO BE GRATEFUL FOR TODAY

Date: /   /

THINGS TO BE GRATEFUL FOR TODAY

> *"Anything worth doing is worth doing well"*
> *— Anonymous*

Date: / /

THINGS TO BE GRATEFUL FOR TODAY

Date: /   /

THINGS TO BE GRATEFUL FOR TODAY

Date: /   /

_____

_____

_____

_____

_____

_____

_____

_____

_____

_____

_____

_____

_____

_____

_____

_____

_____

_____

THINGS TO BE GRATEFUL FOR TODAY

> *"The winner always has a plan; The loser always has an excuse"* — Anonymous

Date: /   /

_____

_____

_____

_____

_____

_____

_____

_____

_____

_____

_____

_____

_____

_____

_____

_____

_____

_____

_____

THINGS TO BE GRATEFUL FOR TODAY

> *"There is no elevator to success.*
> *You have to take the stairs"* — *Anonymous*

Date: /   /

THINGS TO BE GRATEFUL FOR TODAY

> *"Don't let yesterday's disappointments, overshadow tomorrow's achievements"* — *Anonymous*

Date: /   /

_____

_____
_____
_____
_____
_____
_____
_____
_____
_____
_____
_____
_____
_____
_____
_____
_____
_____
_____

THINGS TO BE GRATEFUL FOR TODAY

"We are limited, not by our abilities, but by our vision"
— Anonymous

Date: /   /

THINGS TO BE GRATEFUL FOR TODAY

Date: /   /

THINGS TO BE GRATEFUL FOR TODAY

> *"Happiness is not something you get,*
> *but something you do" — Anonymous*

Date: /   /

THINGS TO BE GRATEFUL FOR TODAY

> *"A journey of a thousand miles must begin with a single step."* – Lao Tzu

Date: ___ / ___ / ___

_____

_____

_____

_____

_____

_____

_____

_____

_____

_____

_____

_____

_____

_____

_____

_____

_____

_____

THINGS TO BE GRATEFUL FOR TODAY

"Try and fail, but don't fail to try" — *Anonymous*

Date: /   /

_____

THINGS TO BE GRATEFUL FOR TODAY

"You risk more when you don't take any risks"

Date: /   /

_____

_____

_____

_____

_____

_____

_____

_____

_____

_____

_____

_____

_____

_____

_____

_____

_____

_____

_____

THINGS TO BE GRATEFUL FOR TODAY

> *"A diamond is a chunk of coal that made good under pressure"* — Anonymous

Date: /   /

_____
_____
_____
_____
_____
_____
_____
_____
_____
_____
_____
_____
_____
_____
_____
_____
_____
_____
_____

THINGS TO BE GRATEFUL FOR TODAY

Date: /   /

_____

THINGS TO BE GRATEFUL FOR TODAY

Date: /   /

_____

_____

_____

_____

_____

_____

_____

_____

_____

_____

_____

_____

_____

_____

_____

_____

_____

THINGS TO BE GRATEFUL FOR TODAY

> *"Remember yesterday, dream of tomorrow,*
> *but live for today"* — Anonymous

Date: /   /

THINGS TO BE GRATEFUL FOR TODAY

"Dream is not what you see in sleep, dream is the thing which does not let you sleep" — Anonymous

Date: /   /

THINGS TO BE GRATEFUL FOR TODAY

> *"Don't be pushed by your problems,*
> *be led by your dreams"* — Anonymous

Date: /   /

_____

THINGS TO BE GRATEFUL FOR TODAY

Date: /   /

THINGS TO BE GRATEFUL FOR TODAY

> *"Once you have a dream put all your heart and soul to achieve it"*

Date: /   /

_____

_____

_____

_____

_____

_____

_____

_____

_____

_____

_____

_____

_____

_____

_____

_____

_____

_____

_____

_____

THINGS TO BE GRATEFUL FOR TODAY

"Follow your heart and your dreams will come true"
– Anonymous

Date: /   /

THINGS TO BE GRATEFUL FOR TODAY

Date: /   /

THINGS TO BE GRATEFUL FOR TODAY

> *"Without dreams you lose interest in life,*
> *you have no energy to move forward"*

Date: /   /

THINGS TO BE GRATEFUL FOR TODAY

"Difficult roads often lead to beautiful destinations"

Date: /   /

_____

THINGS TO BE GRATEFUL FOR TODAY

> *"The road to success is always full of surprises and temporary failures, real success comes to those who persist"*

Date: /   /

_____

_____

_____

_____

_____

_____

_____

_____

_____

_____

_____

_____

_____

_____

_____

_____

_____

_____

_____

THINGS TO BE GRATEFUL FOR TODAY

"Believe in yourself and you will be unstoppable"

Date: /   /

THINGS TO BE GRATEFUL FOR TODAY

> *"Today is another chance to get better"*

Date: /   /

_____

_____

_____

_____

_____

_____

_____

_____

_____

_____

_____

_____

_____

_____

_____

_____

_____

_____

THINGS TO BE GRATEFUL FOR TODAY

"To live a creative life, we must lose our fear of being wrong" - Anonymous

Date: /   /

THINGS TO BE GRATEFUL FOR TODAY

Date: /   /

THINGS TO BE GRATEFUL FOR TODAY

> *"If you do what you always did,*
> *you will get what you always got" - Anonymous*

Date: /   /

THINGS TO BE GRATEFUL FOR TODAY

Date: /   /

THINGS TO BE GRATEFUL FOR TODAY

"You are capable of amazing things"

Date: /   /

THINGS TO BE GRATEFUL FOR TODAY

"Believe in yourself and you will be unstoppable"

Date: /   /

THINGS TO BE GRATEFUL FOR TODAY

"Successful people make a habit of doing what unsuccessful people don't want to do"
– Anonymous

Date: / /

THINGS TO BE GRATEFUL FOR TODAY

Date: /   /

THINGS TO BE GRATEFUL FOR TODAY

"Nothing worth having comes easy" - Anonymous

Date: /   /

THINGS TO BE GRATEFUL FOR TODAY

Date: /   /

THINGS TO BE GRATEFUL FOR TODAY

Date: / /

_____
_____
_____
_____
_____
_____
_____
_____
_____
_____
_____
_____
_____
_____
_____
_____
_____
_____
_____

THINGS TO BE GRATEFUL FOR TODAY

CREATIVE JOURNALS
FACTORY

We hope you enjoyed your journal — notebook,
please let us know if you liked it by writing a review,
it means a lot to us.

Thank you!

Created by: Nice Gifts Press for:

CREATIVE JOURNALS FACTORY

Made in the USA
Monee, IL
03 June 2021

70127373R00063